SELECTED POEMS

SELECTED POEMS

by

ANNA WICKHAM

With an Introduction by
David Garnett

1971
CHATTO & WINDUS
LONDON

Published by
Chatto & Windus Ltd
40 William IV Street
London WC2

∗

Clarke Irwin and Co Ltd
Toronto

ISBN 0 7011 1699 4

**Printed in Great Britain by
Lewis Reprints Limited
London and Tonbridge**

Contents

INTRODUCTION

I was a science student in my second year working in my room late at night when I heard an unknown visitor's voice talking to my parents. It was most unusual for them to have a visitor so late. The voice was a woman's: a rich musical contralto and full of caressing humour. It attracted me so much that I put away my book and went in and joined them. The unknown was a tall, beautiful and powerful woman with shining dark eyes, abundant dark hair parted at the side which fell like a bird's wings over her ears. She had rather heavy features with a warm complexion. She had been singing at the musical evening my father had attended and as it had turned out that she lived a few doors away from us in Downshire Hill, he had invited her in to meet my mother.

While we drank the coffee my mother had prepared, our visitor told us that she had lost her temper with her husband and had been so violent, smashing her hand through a glass door, that he had got a medical friend to bring another doctor and that they had certified her as insane. She had escaped from the house to sing and was now on her way home and expected to be taken to a mental home next morning. She was calm, almost amused, quite sure of herself and not terrified as most people would have been. When she said goodnight, I thrust myself forward and insisted on accompanying her to her doorstep. She did not go in at once and we took a turn to the bottom of the street as far as Hampstead Heath and back while I urged her to hide and asked what I could do to save her. She replied that if she were as sane as she thought, they could not keep her locked up for more than a few weeks. In any case it was for doctors to decide one's sanity — a remark that I thought, and still think, extraordinary.

Next day my mother called but was told that she had gone away for some time. Two months or so later I met

Anna again and she told me that she had taken Hall and Knight's *Algebra* with her and had spent her time in the private asylum working out quadratic equations in order to keep her mind from dwelling on her situation and to overcome her rancour. She had been discharged shortly before the home was due for inspection by visiting doctors.

What she had not told my parents and never told me was the reason for the violent quarrel with her husband, to understand which a knowledge of her background is helpful.

Born in England, she was taken to Australia as a small child. Her father was a rationalist, a piano tuner, a failure in life. Her mother was flamboyant, taught elocution, practised hypnotism and professional character reading. Anna's father encouraged her to write poetry and to become a singer. He longed for her to succeed in the Arts where he had failed. At twenty she came back to England with the twin ambitions of becoming an operatic star and a poet. She was well on her way to success as a singer: de Reszke's favourite pupil, studying under him in Paris, when Patrick Hepburn, a man several years older than herself with a dominating character, persuaded her to marry him. She gave up her musical career and for five years played the difficult role of a model wife to a conventional husband. When the feeling of suffocation became too strong, she began to write poetry in secret:— some of her poems being in unrhymed verse. She sent a few poems to Harold Munro at the Poetry Bookshop. He was greatly interested and published them in a Chapbook. Anna, feeling excited and triumphant, showed them to her husband. He was very angry, thought anything she wrote worthless and in any case had no intention of allowing his wife to be a poet. She was not to do it again. Anna exploded with rage and found herself certified as insane.

After she had been pushed out of the mental home she went back to live with her husband because she was devoted to her sons, then small boys. She was in some ways very proud of her husband. He was an amateur astronomer and

Anna pushed him on to do original work and to get out of the backwater of dabbling in astronomy in his back garden. Eventually he became President of the Royal Astronomical Society, a friend of Jeans and the man who invited Einstein to visit England. He first flew in 1910 and during the 1914-1918 war was a courageous balloonist. But he and Anna were always at odds. On one occasion when he cut off supplies of money she put on a ragged dress and sang to a theatre queue, making a collection of twelve pounds. That defeated him. Many of her poems were written for her to sing. I remember particularly 'The Cherry Blossom Wand':

> So I will drive you, so bewitch your eyes
> With a beautiful thing that shall never grow wise.

We used to go for walks together on Hampstead Heath at night and to meet at the Café Royal and other pubs, and at a nightclub in Greek Street started by Augustus John. At our meetings Anna often pulled pieces of paper out of her bag and passed them over to me. On them were poems she had written since our last meeting. Sometimes something I said struck her and instead of replying she would reach for a pencil, scrawl a few lines and push them across the table. Her answer to my remark was a poem.

I soon realised that her thoughts and feelings were her poems. A stream of good and bad ones flowed through her. Later she might brood over what she had jotted down and if she felt it was what she had wanted to say, she would type it out and preserve it. This method of writing made her poetry a day-to-day record of herself.

The summer after I met her I got to know D.H. Lawrence and Frieda, and talked to Anna about them. She wrote one or two poems based on my anecdotes. 'Imperatrix' was founded on an infidelity of Frieda's:

> Am I pleasant?
> Tell me that, Old Wise!
> Let me look into your eyes,

9

To see if you can comprehend my beauty,
That is a lover's duty.
I look at you to see
If you can think of anything but me.
Ah, you remember praise and your philosophy!
My love shall be a sphere of silence and of light,
Where Love is all alone with love's delight. —
Here is a woodcutter who is so weak
With love of me, he cannot speak.
Tell me, dumb man, am I pleasant, am I pleasant?
Farewell philosopher! I love a peasant.

Later an opportunity came for Anna to get to know Lawrence when he and Frieda were living in The Vale of Health. They went for long walks on the Heath and her sons remember tagging along behind and, after a snowfall, venting their jealousy of the strange man by pelting him with snowballs. A reminiscence of these talks led her to write: 'The Spirit Of The Lawrence Women' which was published in the *Texas Quarterly* (Vol. IX, No. 3, 1966). She was better qualified than many women to understand Lawrence for she had the same Elementary School teacher background as he. Anna showed Lawrence her poetry and he wrote to Eddie Marsh about it in a letter which ends: 'I think some of these poems *very* good. You may like them for Georgian Poetry.'

Anna knew many other poets of course: T.E. Hulme she liked, and thought well of. The 'Song to Amidon' was written for Ezra Pound after she had spent the morning talking to him in Paris.

In the early days most of her friends were artists: Epstein, Augustus John and the tribes of Chelsea, Slade students, their mistresses and models. She preferred the hard-up to the well-off, the doomed and unknown to the rich and successful, Bohemia to Mayfair, Chelsea to Bloomsbury. Anna and I drifted apart. She would not take me as her lover, I was too tidy-minded to like her rag-bag friends and then I became a conscientious objector and she was for the war at the beginning.

In the past I liked her poems because they are so redolent of the warmth, the slow appreciation and humour of the woman I was in love with. Now, reading them after fifty years, I am struck by her individual feeling, her power of putting down no more than she wanted to say, by her avoiding the poetical and conventional and by a felicity of phrase. On the whole I like the unrhymed poems best but a rhymed one, 'The Homecoming', is the most moving of all. Its writing seems like second sight. It is a lament for the death of her husband. But the poem was published in 1921 and Patrick Hepburn was found dead of exposure after a fall while climbing alone in the Lake District in 1929.

DAVID GARNETT

NOTE ON RHYME

Likeness of sound,
With just enough of difference
To make a change of sense;
So we have contrast,
A piquancy,
And a certain victory of contrivance.
But Heaven keep us from an inevitable rhyme,
Or from a rhyme prepared!

Rhymed verse is a wide net
Through which many subtleties escape.
Nor would I take it to capture a strong thing,
Such as a whale.

THE FIRED POT

In our town, people live in rows.
The only irregular thing in a street is the steeple;
And where that points to God only knows,
And not the poor disciplined people!

And I have watched the women growing old,
Passionate about pins, and pence, and soap,
Till the heart within my wedded breast grew cold,
And I lost hope.

But a young soldier came to our town,
He spoke his mind most candidly.
He asked me quickly to lie down,
And that was very good for me.

For though I gave him no embrace —
Remembering my duty —
He altered the expression of my face,
And gave me back my beauty.

EXAMINATION

If my work is to be good,
I must transcend skill, I must master mood.
For the expression of the rare thing in me
Is not in *do,* but deeper, in *to be.*
Something of this kind was meant
When piety was likened to a scent.
A smell is not in movement, not in power,
It is a function of a perfect flower.

I only compass something rare
By the high form of willing which is prayer.
A ship transcendent and a sword of fire,
For me, the traveller, is in desire.
I write my thought in this most ragged way
That, being baulked of beauty, I am stung to pray.

SOUL COLOUR

The only real thing in my garden is the scent of flowers.
Greenness and growth, thorns and the pink,
All colours and shapes are symbols;
They are controlled by the thing they build.

There is no reality in my flesh,
Nor in work, nor in words, nor in possessions;
All these things are symbols of myself,
The sum of emotion, thought and desire,
Which I call soul-colour
And liken to the scent of flowers.

What is this immaculate hat but a symbol of order?
What is money but a symbol of the unattainable,
Or of things within reach?

In life I am like a juggler,
I throw about my symbols, I rearrange them.
I fling my spheres and rings into the air.

There is one reality which is personality,
Which I call soul-colour and liken to a scent.

THE MAN WITH A HAMMER

My Dear was a mason
And I was his stone.
And quick did he fashion
A house of his own.

As fish in the waters,
As birds in a tree,
So natural and blithe lives
His spirit in me.

PARADOX

My brain burns with hate of you.
I am like a green field swept by scorching wind,
Everything withers.
There is nothing left of promise
But black death. Yet in my heart is our eternal love,
Hard and pure as a moonstone,
And like an opal,
Subtle with change.

B

THE CHERRY-BLOSSOM WAND
(To be sung)

I will pluck from my tree a cherry-blossom wand,
And carry it in my merciless hand,
So I will drive you, so bewitch your eyes,
With a beautiful thing that can never grow wise.

Light are the petals that fall from the bough,
And lighter the love that I offer you now;
In a spring day shall the tale be told
Of the beautiful things that will never grow old.

The blossoms shall fall in the night wind,
And I will leave you so, to be kind:
Eternal in beauty are short-lived flowers,
Eternal in beauty, these exquisite hours.

I will pluck from my tree a cherry-blossom wand,
And carry it in my merciless hand,
So I will drive you, so bewitch your eyes,
With a beautiful thing that shall never grow wise.

CREATRIX

Let us thank Almighty God
For the woman with the rod,
Who was ever and is now
Strong, essential as the plough.
She shall goad and she shall drive,
So to keep man's soul alive.
Amoris with her scented dress
Beckons, in pretty wantonness;
But the wife drives, nor can man tell
What hands so urge, what powers compel.

NERVOUS PROSTRATION

I married a man of the Croydon class
When I was twenty-two.
And I vex him, and he bores me
Till we don't know what to do!
It isn't good form in the Croydon class
To say you love your wife,
So I spend my days with the tradesmen's books
And pray for the end of life.

In green fields are blossoming trees
And a golden wealth of gorse,
And young birds sing for joy of worms:
It's perfectly clear, of course,
That it wouldn't be taste in the Croydon class
To sing over dinner or tea:
But I sometimes wish the gentleman
Would turn and talk to me!

But every man of the Croydon class
Lives in terror of joy and speech,
"Words are betrayers," "Joys are brief"
The maxims their wise ones teach.
And for all my labour of love and life
I shall be clothed and fed,
And they'll give me an orderly funeral
When I'm still enough to be dead.

I married a man of the Croydon class
When I was twenty-two.
And I vex him, and he bores me
Till we don't know what to do!
And as I sit in his ordered house,
I feel I must sob or shriek,
To force a man of the Croydon class
To live, or to love, or to speak!

GIFT TO A JADE

For love he offered me his perfect world.
This world was so constricted and so small
It had no sort of loveliness at all,
And I flung back the little silly ball.
At that cold moralist I hotly hurled
His perfect, pure, symmetrical, small world.

SOUL'S LIBERTY

He who has lost soul's liberty
Concerns himself for ever with his property,
As, when the folk have lost both dance and song,
Women clean useless pots the whole day long.

Thank God for war and fire
To burn the silly objects of desire,
That, from the ruin of a church thrown down,
We see God clear and high above the town.

SUSANNAH IN THE MORNING

When first I saw him I was chaste and good,
And he, how ruthless, pardoned not the mood.
From one quick look I knew him dear,
And gave the highest tribute of my fear.
So I played woman to his male:
How better could his power prevail!
But his hot sense showed quick surprise
At the slow challenge of my shaded eyes.
In a closed room what fires may burn!
O my cold lover, will you not return?
To the high night I fling my prayer:
Master of chariots, drive me in the air!

SONG TO AMIDON

Dear Fragrance,
Be no more a man,
But a small hill of herbs.
And I will take you in my hands
And press you to more intimate fine scent;
Then I will hold you to my heart,
Till I know grace.
The hungry winds shall woo me for your sake,
Incontinent, I'll fling you to high air
And you, ascending to poor God's assault,
Shall burden Heaven with your subtle sweet
Till He repents him of old odorous smoke,
And flings out bolts to throw the altars down.

THE SICK ASSAILANT

I hit her in the face because she loved me.
It was the challenge of her faithfulness that moved me.
For she knew me, every impulse, every mood,
As if my veins had run with her heart's blood.
She knew my damned incontinence, my weakness,
Yet she forebore with her accursed meekness.
I could have loved her had she ever blamed me,
It was her sticky irritating patience shamed me.
I was tired-sick. It was her business to amuse me,
Her faith could only daunt me and confuse me.
She was a fine great wench, and well I knew
She was one good half panther, one half shrew,
Then why should my love, more than any other,
Induce in her the silly human Mother?
She would have nursed me, bathed me, fed me, carried me.
She'd have burned her soul to thaw me, she'd have married me.
I hit her in the face because she loved me,
It was her sticky irritating patience moved me.

THE EGOIST

Shall I write pretty poetry —
Controlled by ordered sense in me —
With an old choice of figure and of word,
So call my soul a nesting bird?

Of the dead poets I can make a synthesis,
And learn poetic form that in them is;
But I will use the figure that is real
For me, the figure that I feel.

And now of this matter of ear-perfect rhyme,
My clerk can list all language in his leisure time;
A faulty rhyme may be a well-placed microtone,
And hold a perfect imperfection of its own.

A poet rediscovers all creation;
His instinct gives him beauty, which is sensed relation.
It was as fit for one man's thoughts to trot in iambs
        as it is for me,
Who live not in the horse-age but in the day of aero-
        planes, to write my rhythms free.

THE WINDS

The quality of your rage is my delight,
I saw a wind in a volcanic night
Incline a fir-wood almost to the ground,
And with such strength that I could hear no sound.
So is your anger written for my mind,
In driven trees, and in that mastering wind.

A quality of courage is my gift.
First would you wreck? O Builder, lift
Your hammer against me and strike your fill,
Cleave me to dust, and from that dust my will
Shall rise in spirals, masterful as flame,
Till whirlwinds march in triumphs of your name.

THE WOMAN AND HER INITIATIVE

Give me a deed, and I will give a quality.
Compel this colloid with your crystalline.
Show clear the difference between you and me
By some plain symmetry, some clear stated line.
These bubblings, these half-actions, my revolt from unity.
Give me a deed, and I will show my quality.

THE RESOURCE

When I gave you honest speech
You were annoyed,
When I gave you honest love
Your taste was cloyed.
And now I give you silence,
And a smile you take for chaste.
In these things I am less worthy than a harlot,
And your pride has worked this waste.

THE FAITHFUL AMORIST

Am I not the lover of Beauty
To follow her where I know she is hid
By the aroma of her pleasure?
Yesterday I had pleasure of Helen,
Of white, of yellow hair;
But to-day a negress is my delight,
And Beauty is black.

There are some that are as small tradesmen,
To sell beauty in a shop,
Noting what has been desired, and acclaiming it
  eternally good.
So poets fill verses
For ever with the owl, the oak, and the nightingale;
I say the crow is a better bird than the nightingale,
Since to-day Beauty is black.

The lark sings flat
Of wearisome trees and spiritless fields;
But there is great music in the hyena,
For there is pleasure in deserts.

SELF ANALYSIS

The tumult of my fretted mind
Gives me expression of a kind;
But it is faulty, harsh, not plain —
My work has the incompetence of pain.

I am consumed with slow fire,
For righteousness is my desire;
Towards that good goal I cannot whip my will,
I am a tired horse that jibs upon a hill.

I desire Virtue, though I love her not —
I have no faith in her when she is got:
I fear that she will bind and make me slave,
And send me songless to the sullen grave.

I am like a man who fears to take a wife,
And frets his soul with wantons all his life.
With rich, unholy foods I stuff my maw;
When I am sick, then I believe in law.

I fear the whiteness of straight ways —
I think there is no colour in unsullied days.
My silly sins I take for my heart's ease,
And know my beauty — in the end — disease.

Of old there were great heroes, strong in fight,
Who, tense and sinless, kept a fire alight:
God of our hope, in their great name,
Give me the straight and ordered flame.

VOCATION

I will walk always at your left hand
To have my right hand nearest to your heart,
That from your love I ask and understand
How best the power in me can play its part.

Discover in the stillness of your soul
What, for your purpose, you most need of me.
You are my hands' work, and my just control,
That is my happy destiny.

SONG

I will sing no more of Love
Love shall sing in me.
I will sing the bird in the grove,
The flower the fish and the bee.
For I love well small things that dwell
On land and in the sea.

DOMESTIC ECONOMY

I will have few cooking-pots,
They shall be bright,
They shall reflect to blinding
God's straight light.
I will have four garments,
They shall be clean,
My service shall be good,
Though my diet be mean.
Then I shall have excess to give the poor,
And right to counsel beggars at my door.

EXPLANATION

It's so, good Sirs, a Woman-poet sings,
Sick self, and not exterior things,
She'd joy enough in flowers, and lakes and light,
Before she won soul's freedom in a fight.
Thus half creation is but half expressed,
And the unspoken half is best

Note

It will be seen this fact is stated,
Of such intrepid artists as are mated;
A maid, good Sirs, in many senses human,
As artist is a negligible woman.

SONG

I was so chill and overworn and sad,
To be a lady was the only joy I had.
I walked the street as silent as a mouse,
Buying fine clothes, and fittings for the house.

But since I saw my love
I wear a simple dress,
And happily I move,
Forgetting weariness.

PERSONALITY

A perfect small creature sat singing in a bubble
This was his magical house.
Beetles and flying-things led the assault against it;
They strove to enter the frail walls,
Pressing their black forefeet against an iridescence.

The song of the small creature
Controlled the invaders.
A weight of singing thrown against the walls
Kept the enemy from entering.

When the singer sings no longer,
The house shall fall.

DEAR BIRD OF WINTER

Dear bird of winter,
On a blue bush,
Translated mavis — marvellous late thrush,
Young wagtail for your swaying lovely walk,
Wren for your heart, and ring-dove for your talk.
Live always in a quality of words
More apt — more swift
More excellent than birds.

c

Alas! for all the pretty women who marry dull men,
Go into the suburbs and never come out again,
Who lose their pretty faces and dim their pretty eyes,
Because no one has skill or courage to organize.

What do these pretty women suffer when they marry?
They bear a boy who is like Uncle Harry,
A girl who is like Aunt Eliza, and not new,
These old dull races must breed true.

I would enclose a common in the sun,
And let the young wives out to laugh and run;
I would steal their dull clothes and go away,
And leave the pretty naked things to play.

Then I would make a contract with hard Fate
That they see all the men in the world and choose a mate,
And I would summon all the pipers in the town
That they dance with Love at a feast, and dance him down.

From the gay unions of choice
We'd have a race of splendid beauty and of thrilling voice.
The World whips frank, gay love with rods,
But frankly gaily shall we get the gods.

THE TIRED MAN

I am a quiet gentleman,
And I would sit and dream;
But my wife is on the hillside,
Wild as a hill-stream.

I am a quiet gentleman,
And I would sit and think;
But my wife is walking the whirlwind
Through night as black as ink.

O, give me a woman of my race
As well controlled as I,
And let us sit by the fire,
Patient till we die!

THE HARE

Love, love, the dogs are after me,
I am transmuted to a white hare.
You sit in the lighted house and cannot see,
I know that you are there.
See where I pass, a shadow on the grass,
Come swiftly
Lift me to your care.

SONG OF OPHELIA THE SURVIVOR

There is no smirch of sin in you only its fires,
You are a man burned white with merciless desires,
A restless heat consumes you, and your brain
Tortured to torturing craves for ugly pain.

Beauty still lives in you and from her seat
Controls your glances and directs your feet,
One look from you taught me so much of love,
I have all pleasure just to watch you move.

That look was like a wet blue mist of flowers
Which held compelling loveliness and sleepy powers.
I dreamed of calling pipes down a warm glade,
By the transposed music of your soul was I betrayed.

Pipe for me, my dear lover. I will come
And your sick soul shall find in me a home,
I will be your house clean, high and strong
And you shall live in me all winter long.

As you are fevered, I will be a pool
Full of green shadows level, silent, cool,
You shall bathe in me, in my being move;
I will put out your fires with my strong love.

A thousand changes shall my love reveal
And all its changes shall have power to heal,
And in the end we'll be as we began:
I will be simple woman, you my man.

A LOVE LETTER

You have given me some quality of the male,
While I have given you some qualities of myself.
You are the father of my action,
While I have begotten in you new courage.
Maybe we are completed by love,
So that we are beyond sex.
We have found the miraculous unity,
To which existence itself implies increase.

I do not grieve away my days
Because you are gone from me,
My mind is stimulated forever by the idea of you,
I do not ask that your love should be faithful to my body,
It is impossible that your soul should be faithless to my soul.

It is well I cannot eat with you all my days,
I would not take my soup from a consecrated cup.
I have before me a wealth of happy moments when I shall
    see you.
They are like holy wafers, which I will eat,
For stimulation, for absolution, and for my eternal hope.

I ask nothing of you, not even that you live,
If you die, I remember you
Till the blood in my wrists is cold.

THE FREE INTELLIGENCE

When I put off the sense in death,
And lose all seeming with my breath,
I will not heed the prejudice of nose,
Comparisons of carrion and rose.

When this now fettered judgment shall be free,
All changes are of equal worth to me.
And I will pleasure in the faultless way
My flesh dissolves to worms and fertile clay.

SENTIMENTS

Windswept from where they grew
These tender flowers lie dead:
How many things were true
Had they been left unsaid.

THE MILL

I hid beneath the covers of the bed,
And dreamed my eyes were lovers
On a hill that was my head.
They looked upon the loveliest country I have seen,
Great fields of red-brown earth hedged round with green.
In these enclosures I could see
The high perfection of fertility.
I knew there were sweet waters near to feed the land,
I heard the churning of a mill on my right hand,
I woke to breathlessness with a quick start
And found my mill the beating of your heart.

INVITATION TO TEA

How cruelly you come my way —
Enough to fill my aching day
With ghosts of singing.
Rhythms unfulfilled
By any tone of meaning
I have willed.

Be more a niggard — or much less,
Cure me with famine or excess.
Let full eclipse repose my sight,
Or honest shining give me light,
To set your beauty
Where it most belongs
Within the outline
Of my shadow songs.

THE AVENUE

To the tired traveller in summer's heat,
The thought of airy trees is sweet.
Come, in my straight, stretched arms discover
A leafy road, thou weary Lover.

THE SLIGHTED LADY

There was a man who won a beautiful woman.
Not only was she lovely, and shaped like a woman,
But she had a beautiful mind.
She understood everything the man said to her,
She listened and smiled,
And the man possessed her and grew in ecstasy,
And he talked while the woman listened and smiled.

But there came a day when the woman understood even
      more than the man had said;
Then *she* spoke, and the man, sated with possession, and
      weary with words, slept.
He slept on the threshold of his house.
The woman was within, in a small room.

Then to the window of her room
Came a young lover with his lute,
And thus he sang:

"O, beautiful woman, who can perfect my dreams,
Take my soul into your hands
Like a clear crystal ball.
Warm it to softness at your breast,
And shape it as you will.
We two shall sing together living songs,
And walk our Paradise in an eternal noon —
Come, my Desire, I wait."

But the woman, remembering the sleeper and her faith,
Shook her good head to keep the longing from her eyes,
At which the lover sang again, and with such lusty rapture
That the sleeper waked,
And, listening to the song, he said:
"My woman has bewitched this man —
He is seduced.

What folly does he sing?
This woman is no goddess, but my wife;
And no perfection, but the keeper of my house."

Whereat the woman said within her heart;
"My husband has not looked at me for many days —
He has forgot that flesh is warm,
And that the spirit hungers.
I have waited long within the house;
I freeze with dumbness, and I go."

Then she stept down from her high window
And walked with her young lover, singing to his lute.

THE SONG OF THE CHILD

Receive me again, Father God,
There is no room!
There is war upon earth, men fight,
They have no time, no food, no pity for babes.
The women staunch men's wounds, and forget us.
Mothers with child are starved.
The new-born dies at the empty breast;
So I died who was your messenger.
I have made no beauty, I have spoke no truth,
I have failed, I was rejected, born too soon,
Receive me again! Father God! Receive me!

THE CHILD AT THE BREAST

See the little Trumpeter
Blowing to the world's heart.
O mothers and O fathers!
Carry me to the gates of your dreams
For I am the inheritor,
I am that man Love has set in life.

THE FOUNDLING

There is a little naked child at the door,
His name is Beauty, and he cries:
"Behold, I am born, put me where I can live."
The old World comes to the door,
And thrusting out a lip, says only this:
"It is true that you are born, but how were you
        conceived?"

There is an owl upon an elder-tree
Who, opening an eye, says only this:
"That is a lovely child!"
The old World said again:
"Yes! but how was he conceived?"

There is a gust of free wind,
And high cloud voices call:
"What can you ask of Love but conception?
Men are born of blest love,
Of evil love is death.
There is but one pure love, the love of Child,
And that is sweet as a pine forest, clean as the sea:
Old World, take all your children in."

TWO EGOTISTS

Two men lived together in a house.
One walked in a sphere of silence,
The other filled all spaces with his talk.
This was well,
For the first feared even to listen to his own silence,
And the second had use for all the words in the world,
And for still more words.

The talker was busy with interpretation.
He watched life, and was interested in himself
As the live thing of which he had most knowledge.
He looked at himself, as a man might look at a hill,
Expounding himself, as one might expound
The phenomena of rain and cloud.

He said: "I am a fine fellow because life is a fine thing,
And I tell you this splendid story of myself,
Because you too are a fine fellow, and know how to
    laugh."
There was a day when the silent man,
Opening his mouth like a lizard who prepares to take
    food, said:
"You talk too much."

Then the talker said:
"I am interested in myself, because I am the live thing
    of which I know most,
And I am interested in you, because you are a man
Of whom I know much,
And I think what you say is probably true;
And, as far as is conformable with growth,
I will talk less."
But he still talked a great deal.
He ranged earth and sky,
And one day in talk he turned to consider the silent man.

He said: "It seems to me, my friend, that you do too little,
You are not busy because you are silent,
In order for you to be silent,
It is necessary for you to keep quite still."

The silent man said:
"In this sphere of mine is perfect order."

The talker said:
"There is no growth in perfection
The perfect thing is still,
And, in a moving world, the still thing dies.

Outside your order there are burdened women,
Sick children, and workless men.
It seems to me, that there are burdened women
Sick children and workless men
Because of your order.

Your race made you, and the world feeds you.
Sing a little song, O my brother,
A small disorderly song."

But the silent man's mouth snapt to
Like a lizard's after he has taken food
And a look came into his eyes of ravished instinct.
He got up quite quietly and killed the talker.
After which he lived vehemently,
Still silent.

THE HOMECOMING

I waited ten years in the husk
That once had been our home,
Watching from dawn to dusk
To see if he would come.

And there he was beside me
Always at board and bed;
I looked — and woe betide me
He I had loved was dead.

He fell at night on the hillside,
They brought him home to his place,
I had not the solace of sorrow
Till I had looked at his face.

Then I clasped the broken body
To see if it breathed or moved,
For there, in the smile of his dying,
Was the gallant man I had loved.

O wives come lend me your weeping,
I have not enough of tears,
For he is dead who was sleeping
These ten accursed years.

ENVOI

God, thou great symmetry
Who put a biting lust in me
From whence my sorrows spring,
For all the frittered days
That I have spent in shapeless ways
Give me one perfect thing.